Dick Sing Turns Miniature Birdhouses

NORTHWEST WASHINGTON
WOODTURNERS ASSOCIATION

Text written with and photography by Donna S. Baker

Schiffer Publishing Ltd

4880 Lower Valley Road, Atglen, PA 19310 USA

Dedication

Over the many years of rubbing elbows with some of the greatest turners in the world, I would like to give them my thanks. I have learned from each and every turner that I have ever met. Not always what to do, but occasionally what not to do. My whole turning world has been shaped by watching, remembering, and at times utilizing new methods. When I first started turning, there were very few books, demonstrations, symposiums, or chances to learn. Bummer!!! The newcomer to turning now has a multitude of options in which to expand his or her knowledge. I hope they appreciate the opportunities they have in front of them and utilize them to the utmost. I still take advantage of them at every opportunity.

As to the birdhouses, Robert Rosand, Dale Nish, and many more have preceded me. I only hope I can represent my turnings on a par with them. I thank Dale Nish for being a mentor, for borrowing a few of his ideas, and for the sharing of his friendship.

And last but not least, to Cindy, my wife, the one who shares my joys and tribulations. The one who helps me form my ideas and words when writing my books and who also sets up a mean gallery. The one whom I would be lost without. My best friend.

Copyright © 2004 by Dick Sing
Library of Congress Card Number: 2004105533

Designed by Joseph M. Riggio Jr.
Gallery set-up by Cindy Sing.
Type set in Americana XBd BT/Korinna BT

ISBN: 0-7643-2080-7
Printed in China

Published by Schiffer Publishing Ltd.
4880 Lower Valley Road
Atglen, PA 19310
Phone: (610) 593-1777; Fax: (610) 593-2002
E-mail: Info@schifferbooks.com

For the largest selection of fine reference books on this and related subjects, please visit our web site at
www.schifferbooks.com
We are always looking for people to write books on new and related subjects. If you have an idea for a book please contact us at the above address.

This book may be purchased from the publisher.
Include $3.95 for shipping.
Please try your bookstore first.
You may write for a free catalog.

In Europe, Schiffer books are distributed by
Bushwood Books
6 Marksbury Ave.
Kew Gardens
Surrey TW9 4JF England
Phone: 44 (0) 20 8392-8585; Fax: 44 (0) 20 8392-9876
E-mail: info@bushwoodbooks.co.uk
Free postage in the U.K., Europe; air mail at cost.

Contents

Introduction

Miniature birdhouses are fun. They can be traditional or whimsical miniature works of art. They are great for utilizing all of those little odd bits of wood you could not bear to throw out or part with. Being small and delicate, they will help your tool control improve, as they are finesse turnings. A quality birdhouse can take as much time or more than a bowl to turn.

Having turned a few birdhouses, they immediately stirred my creative juices. As I demonstrate, I am always in need of new subject matter. Birdhouses have always been of interest to both men and women, so I thought I would add them to my program. I decided my houses needed my own set of standards. They needed to have an undercut eave, as many other birdhouses do not. I wanted them to be light in weight and I also wanted repeatability; in other words, I wanted them to have interchangeable parts (to a point). Therefore, I now have a modern day version of Mr. Potato Head. This is very handy, as if my original idea of what should go with what does not enthuse me I can swap different roofs with different bodies, etc. Upon finishing, this gives me the leeway of change and variety.

A common misconception is that a small object is easier to turn than a large one. Not true! Both have their own quirks and problems. The smaller the turning the more problematic it becomes. Smaller means you need a more delicate touch and precise tool control, with many mistakes becoming a disaster. Sharp tools are a necessity for cutting with less pressure. Heavy-handedness causes vibration, which can cause catches, poor surfaces, etc.

There are many ways to hold the work piece. Mine is not the only way. Some of the methods I started with I have already dropped by the wayside. Ideas and methods change with necessity, along with improvement. As you extend your quest for the perfect birdhouse, you will encounter problems. It may be with holding the work piece, turning, finishing techniques, or whatever. Don't give up. Think your way out of it. That's how improvement is gained and knowledge is learned. Do your best. Being a small object, the birdhouse does not warrant anything less than your best effort. And most important, this is supposed to be fun. Keep it that way. I hope you enjoy the book.

Chapter One
The Basic Birdhouse

A basic birdhouse is easy to start on and will help you gain confidence along with learning how to hold the work pieces. Worry about the razzmatazz later…crawl before walking.

Most turners have a desire to turn the most beautiful woods into a breathtaking culmination or grand finale on their first attempt. Get real – it won't happen. A sound piece of available stock on hand will be sufficient. Every time you make a new project you should strive to make a better finished piece. It is a rare individual who can make a heart-fluttering presentation on his first try. Kudos are earned, not given like merit badges. Learn the ropes, give of your soul, be human.

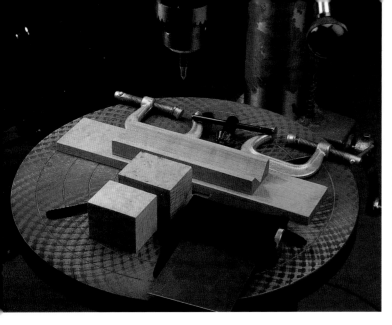

For the basic house, I am going to use maple burl—it's not my first attempt. The house body measures approximately 1-1/2" square and 1-3/4" to 2" long. The roof measures 1-3/4" square and 2-1/4" long. These dimensions can be adjusted to your preference of shape or the material available.

Select the surface that you feel would present the best appearance for the opening of the birdhouse. With the block being square, you have four choices. For the first step, draw the centerline of your block.

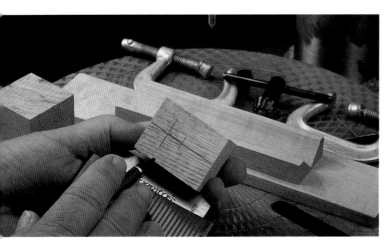

Now lay out the cross lines for the entry hole and the perch hole. Mine are approximately 1/2" below the top of the house for the entry hole and 1" below the top for the perch hole. I like to keep the nicest grain pattern at the top, as most of the wood is removed from the bottom on this shape.

Drilling the holes in line is important, as any misalignment on such a small object really shows up. For the basic house, I'll use a very simple but effective setup. Using a straightedge (I'm using the edge of a vee block), align your centerline directly underneath the quill. In the chuck, I use a centerfinder (a piece of metal that has been concentrically ground to a sharp point) or a small diameter drill. With the block tight against the straightedge, you should be directly on the centerline. Clamp your straightedge to the drill press table.

The hole size is not mandatory. My entry hole on this house happens to be 1/4" diameter. Make sure when you locate the block against the straightedge there are no shavings or foreign matter to cause misalignment. This is especially important as you want to keep both holes on the same centerline. Drill the holes deep enough to be able to shape the body without losing the hole — 3/8" to 1/2" or whatever. Centerline would be maximum depth.

I use a 1/8" diameter hole for the perch.

I have mounted the block into a four jaw chuck with the top of the house towards the tailstock.

Starting to shape the body of the house.

After rough shaping the body, it is time to drill. I have installed a 3/4" dia. Fostner bit to drill out the bulk of the body. This will also establish a dimensional hole at the top of the body. As you notice, on the shank of the drill bit are white and orange pieces of tape. Since most lathes do not have a scale on the quill of the tailstock, I have these established for different lengths so I can measure easily, just by looking. The white tape is set at 3/4" depth and the orange is 1" in depth. The back side of the orange would be 1-1/4" depth. They can be set to whatever your needs may warrant.

All wood lathe tailstocks have a certain amount of side-to-side play. If the tailstock were locked down in its most out of alignment position, we would drill an oversized hole. What I like to do is leave the tailstock loose, advancing it by hand slowly into the work piece with the lathe running. As the point of the drill contacts the rotating work piece, it will automatically center the tailstock as best as possible. When that happens, I lock down the tailstock. At this point, I drill.

I am drilling my hole 1-1/4" deep with the 5/8" dia. Fostner. This creates a stepped hole, which will be used to help locate it on a mandrel. It also allows me to make the bottom of the house smaller in diameter. If I had used the 3/4" dia. to the bottom, I would end up with a basic straight-sided house.

I am drilling the hole about 7/8" deep.

I've changed to a 5/8" dia. Fostner bit in the drill chuck. I have put tape on this bit as well, with the start of the white tape at 1-1/4", start of the orange tape at 1-3/8", and the ending point at 1-5/8".

Now that we have established our hole at the top of the body, we can true up the outer shape, except for the area being held in the chuck. Work close to the jaws but be careful not to contact them. We will have to "guesstimate" the finished shape of this area. Be sure to check the surface for cracks, voids, or any other defects. Cracks can be glued with thin viscosity cyanoacrylate (superglue), while voids can be filled with shavings or dust and flooded with cyanoacrylate. In the course of this book, we are bound to come across a situation such as this and we will discuss it at length then. Read on...

We have roughed out the shape desired, so it's time to hollow out the interior. I have removed the tailstock to allow myself working room. A 1/4" square round nose scraper will be my tool of choice for the hollowing. The reason we are doing this is to make the body as light in weight as possible. Preserve approximately 1/8" of the original 3/4" diameter drilled hole and, as you hollow, do not cut out all of the 5/8" diameter hole. These dimensioned holes will be used when we reverse the body and place it on a mandrel.

True up the top of the body. I am using a 3/8" spindle gouge in a shear cut mode. Then remove the block from the chuck.

The hollowing in progress.

Determining the wall thickness is easy, as all you have to do is look through the entry hole. Leave enough wall thickness that you can finish off the outside shape when reversed. Check at the bottom to make sure you have left enough of the 5/8" diameter hole that is not damaged for mounting purposes. If you have destroyed this, redrill the 5/8" diameter hole a little deeper.

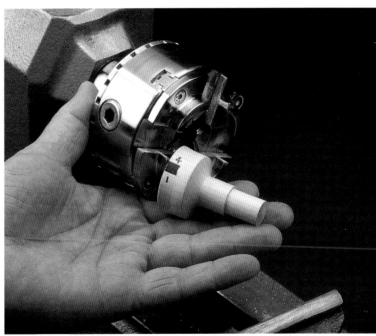

To reverse the body and finish the outside and the bottom, we will need a means of holding the work piece. We are going to use a shop made wooden mandrel. To make this mandrel, I used a piece of hard maple approximately 1-3/4" diameter by 2-1/2" long. I cleaned up the surface that will be held in the chuck, turned it around, and clamped it into the chuck. I have a habit of marking my scrap blocks and mandrels so they can be repositioned into the chuck at any time. To do this, I clamp them tightly in the chuck, release them, and retighten. The density of the wood is not uniform. By tightening and retightening, the fibers are compressed to conform to the chuck. By marking a certain jaw, you can reposition it with relative concentricity.

After mounting the mandrel in the chuck, create a shoulder at the tailstock end that is 5/8" diameter by 3/4" long. Adjacent to the headstock end, create a 3/4" diameter by 3/4" long area. These will match the holes drilled in the body, allowing us to reverse the body. This must be done with precision, as the mandrel will hold the body concentric to the lathe and use a friction fit to drive it. These mandrels can be made in a multitude of sizes – use whatever fits your needs. I take as much care as I can making mine as I reuse them many times.

Slide the body onto the mandrel. If the mandrel was made properly and the holes were drilled properly, it will be a friction fit and run true.

Bring your tailstock up against the bottom of the body to help support the turning. I am using an extended point on my live center. This is not essential, but since I have the ability to change points in my live center by using the extended point of a small diameter tip, it just gives me more room to work. If yours has a fixed point, use that. I am reducing the diameter that had been in the chuck.

Starting to develop the shape on the bottom of the body.

Shortening up the body of the house. My eye felt that I could reduce the overall height of the body and I had enough extra stock in the bottom to do this.

Finishing the outside shape of the body.

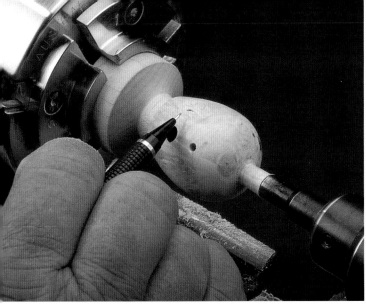

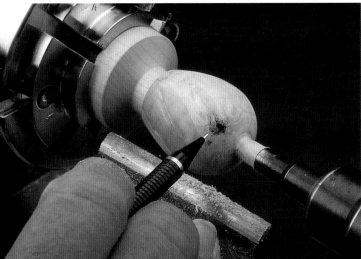

As luck would have it, we have uncovered a small void and a bark inclusion.

Using the thin cyanoacrylate, flood the wood dust in the void and the bark inclusion. You can hit the wet glue with accelerator to immediately cure the glue, but use caution: if the area is very large or the void is deep, or if too much of the cyanoacrylate has been used, it will react with a lot of heat and set off a white contaminant. If this occurs below your finished surface, you will never get it out. Waiting a few minutes will normally allow the glue to cure on its own. If not, apply the accelerator at that point and the curing will not be as violent as with freshly applied glue.

Around the toolrest, you will normally find some very fine shavings and dust. These can be used to fill the voids. Pack the fine dust or shavings into these areas.

Using a very light cut or a shear cut, clean up the surface.

I've patched it and cleaned it up and am satisfied with the results.

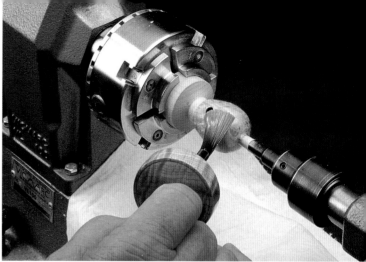

The finish that I use is Deft™ satin finish. I use it straight out of the can and keep a small amount in a brush-in-jar of my own making. This makes it easy to apply. Also, when using some woods, the dust contaminates the finish. For example, cocobolo dust will turn clear finish a reddish orange. Since my bottle contains only a small amount of finish, I do not have a problem throwing it away and refilling the jar if necessary. I always protect my lathe from any dripping finish by covering the ways with a paper towel. A clean lathe is always a nicer tool to work on.

Time to sand. I started with 240 grit. The starting grit depends on the surface you are going to finish. If your surface is extremely rough or torn, you may need to start with a coarser grit. If you need 36 grit to clean up the surface, I think you better recut it. I've worked my way through 240, 320, 400, and 600 grits. Do not hold your sandpaper in one spot – always keep it moving. If it's held in one place, you will sometimes cut grooves, which we are trying to eliminate.

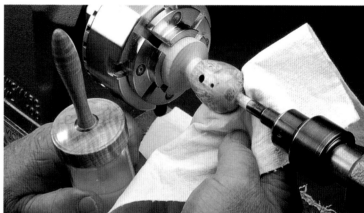

I normally allow the Deft™ to soak in for a few minutes before buffing it off with a paper towel. Occasionally, I will immediately put on a second coat. Here's a good view of the finish jar, too.

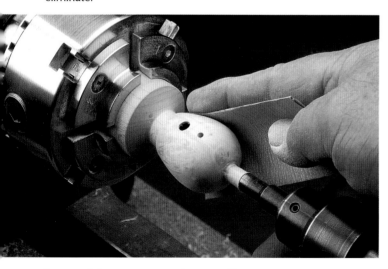

I contend that you cannot eliminate all concentric scratches with the lathe running. Therefore, my final preparation is with the lathe off and hand sanding.

Using a parting tool, cut off most of the excess from the base of the body.

Using a 3/16" drill, drill a hole in the base for the finial.

Determine which end of the roof block you would like to match to the body. In other words, if there are any defects that can be turned away, use that end as the top of the roof. Once determining this, you want to have the base of the roof pointed away from the chuck, i.e., towards the tailstock. Tighten down the piece in the chuck.

Using a gouge, clean up the very bottom of the body. I like to concave the base slightly, so that when the finial is installed it only contacts around the edge to make a nice mating surface.

Clean up the diameter.

Our body is complete.

When your diameter is cleaned up, start to create a tenon that will hold the body. This tenon will be a friction fit. The reason that I attach the roof to the body using a tenon in this manner is so I can create an undercut eave. It also allows me to use another jig to reverse the roof.

Work the tenon down towards the size you need and deepen it to create the eave.

With the body attached, you can determine the diameter you want for the roof in order to make it proportional.

Use the body to determine the fit. Use care, as we want this to be a snug fit.

With the body still attached, turn the roof diameter until your eye tells you it is the right proportion.

When I am very close, I use a small parting tool to cut a flat spot that will match the top of the body. The snug fit of the tenon, and the mating of the top of the body to that flat surface, will make everything mesh together in concentric alignment.

Now that we have determined the diameter of the roof, we can finish the underside. Don't take too much off the top of the roof, as you need that material for stabilization while cutting.

Using a shear cut, clean up the underside of the roof to your satisfaction.

Since we are trying to make a very light birdhouse, take the tip of a gouge, find the exact center of the piece, and push it forward like a drill. Pull it out in a pull cut and you will remove some of the excess weight from the roof.

As you did with the body, sand out the underside of the roof. Do not sand the tenon, however, as that will disturb the fit between the body and the roof.

Using the Deft™, finish the entire underside.

The underside has been finished and the fit is good. We are ready to continue working on the roof.

Using a small parting tool, you can either cut the roof off or – to conserve as much of the wood for design possibilities (which I like to do) – cut through the end of the block and maintain the full length. The configuration of the jaws on your chuck may not allow you to do this; mine does allow this operation. If you're unsure, it's best not to try, as the noise of the parting tool getting caught in the base of the jaws makes a horrible racket. Better safe than sorry.

Removing stock from the peak of the roof.

To reverse the roof, I use a friction fit jig. The same tenon that holds the body, which should be a 3/4" diameter dimensioned hole, will now fit inside an appropriate hole in a scrap block to hold and drive the roof. A jig made totally of wood works fine. I have used them often, especially while demonstrating, but I felt I wanted something more durable. I have inserted a piece of PVC pipe into my wooden scrap block. In this picture, the one on the right is wood and the one on the left is the combination PVC and wood. When I size the ID (inside dimension) of the jig, I normally bore it with a square edge scraper, rather than drilling it, to establish a slightly tighter fit. With the scraper, I have more control over the cut and can adjust the tightness of the fit by making a slightly smaller hole. The drill, on the other hand, shows no mercy because it cuts a fixed diameter.

The small flat next to the tenon, which we worked so hard to get to match the top of the body, is now going to rest against the flat surface of our PVC jig. Make sure that jig surface is true, as again the diameter and the mating of those surfaces will keep everything concentric – and thus help to create the best hold.

There are a couple of bark inclusions that I'm hoping will cut out. Occasionally, bark inclusions will not be adhered to the rest of the wood and have a tendency to pop out as you are turning. As a preventive measure, I am going to flood these with the thin cyanoacrylate, just to make sure they stay put.

Starting to shape our roof.

I've pressed and seated the roof onto the jig, spun it, and made sure it ran true. I've brought up the tailstock and live center to give stability while I cut.

That bark inclusion that we already glued has a void underneath it. I'm still hoping I'll be able to turn it out. If not, we may need a design modification. Continue roughing in the shape of your roof. The band in the center will become a bead, and I have left it large enough that I can move it higher or lower on the roof to satisfy my eye.

I had to trim a little off the height of the roof to eliminate part of that bark inclusion.

I normally buy a length of 1/8" dowel and cut it into shorter lengths as needed. We all know 1/8" dowels are never a perfect 1/8". I like to sand it to a loose fit so it can be glued in easily. To hold the dowel, I just stick it in the hole and lightly sand it. If necessary, reverse the dowel and sand the opposite end as well.

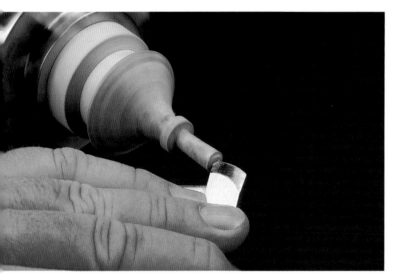

I trimmed off the top of the roof mainly to eliminate a bad spot. After trimming it off, however, I think the height looks better anyway. Learn to use your eye. Burl is not always a strong wood. With the grain going in all directions, and with occasional voids or defects, we stand a good chance of breaking our roof when going down to a small diameter. Therefore, I like to strengthen any suspect roof by gluing a 1/8" dowel down the middle. To do so, we must first drill a 1/8" hole. All drills have a tendency to go in the direction of least resistance, so to help start the drill to the best advantage, I take the tip of a skew and establish a small indentation on centerline. Once the drill is started, we have no control over its course of direction to a point, but we can do everything to make sure it starts correctly.

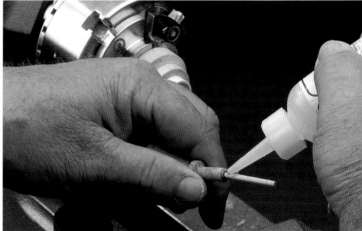

To glue the dowel in, start by getting everything you need ready in advance. Remove the roof from the jig. Why? One time, I removed the chuck with the roof attached in the jig and did my gluing that way, so as not lose any concentricity. Unfortunately, the glue went all the way down the hole and glued the roof to the jig. Yes, this is a word to the wise from experience! Start by applying a drop of the thin cyanoacrylate down the hole, insert the dowel lightly and apply some of the medium density cyanoacrylate, then rotate the dowel as you seat it…this spreads the glue. You can apply a little accelerator and you're ready to reinstall the roof on the jig. Make sure the tenon and the little flat are clean so they reseat properly on the jig.

The drilling of the hole is straightforward. Be careful to clean the chips out often, as your roof is held on by friction only. The depth can be all the way through if necessary or at least into a heavier portion of the roof.

Using a small gouge, trim off the excess dowel and again, take the point of the skew and mark a small indentation in the very center.

I've determined where I want my bead and have started to form it.

We need to have a means of holding the entire birdhouse up when finished. For the eyelet that we'll use later, I need to predrill a 1/16" hole that the eyelet can be threaded into. To do so, I use a small pin vise that I've put in a wooden handle. Take the tip of a skew and make a small indentation at center line. Looking down at the bed of the lathe, align the drill and pin vise and place the tip of the drill in the indentation. If the tip of the drill is running true, i.e., not wobbling, you can advance it forward and drill a hole with more control than if the drill were in the tailstock. Naturally, if the tip of the drill is *not* holding true in that indentation, something's wrong and you have no idea where the drill going to go. In that case, recut the indentation, making sure it is true. When I make a roof without a dowel, but using wood with angular grain, at times the 1/16" drill has a mind of its own – it will follow the direction of least resistance or follow the grain direction. On the other hand, if you wait to drill that eyelet hole until after finishing the roof, it will sometimes not be centered because of following the grain. By drilling the hole *before* we finish turning the roof, and by locating the live center in that hole, the roof will be turned concentric to the hole. Naturally this refers to only small errors in alignment.

When creating a small bead, sometimes the pores in the wood are large enough to be cracks. To help prevent the bead from coming apart, I like to flood it with the thin cyanoacrylate. This permeates the cracks, pores, and any imperfections, and makes the wood as solid as possible.

Working to get the proper shape for our roof.

Upon getting my shape close to the desired result, my eye told me that the top was still too long. I therefore cut off a small amount and repositioned my tailstock. Working the small diameter section, of course, we are limited as to how small we can go. We do not want to expose the reinforcing dowel.

This will be strictly a light finishing cut. All the major material was removed beforehand with a gouge. Too heavy a cut will produce chattering, seeing how the piece is very thin, and would probably snap the small diameter section even though it has a reinforcing dowel in it. Finesse is the word. You can see I am considerably above centerline, which is not a normal scrape. Also, notice the shape of the cutting edge and how it allows me to blend a nice radius on the roof.

For my finishing cut, I am going to use a scraper that I have modified. It is ground similarly to a skew, only a little more acute and in the shape of a French curve. If I had ground it to a normal scraper angle, I don't feel it would be as sharp or as strong. A long tapered grind would not give sufficient strength, compared to the double grind that I have. The only difference is, I have to drop my handle down and put one of the ground surfaces 90 degrees to the work.

Finish the bead and we'll be ready to sand.

As you can see, the toolrest is considerably below centerline, which puts my handle low and my cutting edge slightly higher than in a normal scraper mode.

Sanding through our normal grits. As you can see, I'm sanding up to the bead but not over it. If you take the time to put in detail, take the time to protect it while sanding.

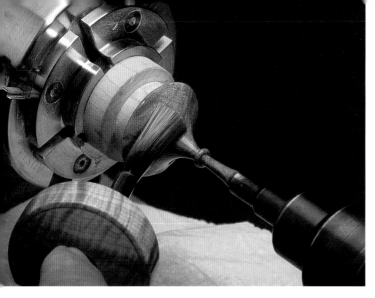

Apply your Deft™ finish and buff dry.

I have changed the jaws on my chuck to make it more convenient for me. If you do not have long nosed jaws per se, just use what you have. I have also removed the live center from the tailstock. Whenever the tailstock is not in use, clear it out…blood from wounds has a tendency to be corrosive on the ways of the lather. Protect that lathe! I have put in a piece of coco bolo (a pen blank) from which I will turn the bottom finial and perch.

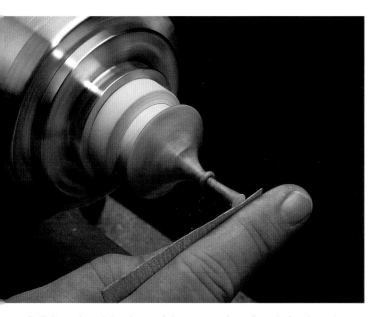

Pull the tailstock back, sand the very end, and apply finish to that area.

Reducing the square blank to a round. I'm using a skew with a paring cut. Use whatever tool you are most comfortable with – a gouge is the one most typically used.

Install the eyelet. I use a number 216-1/2 brass eyelet. As you can see, our eyelet is centered to the roof. At this stage, we are done with the roof.

I decided a ball type finial would look best and am starting to form the ball. I am using a 1/4" spindle gouge.

Continuing to form the ball.

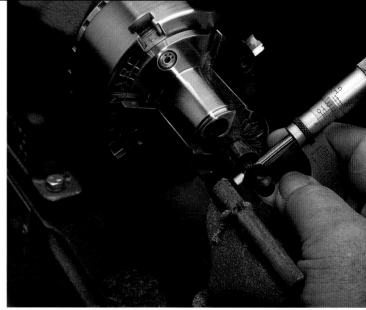

I have completed the tenon. For measuring small diameters, I use a micrometer. Most of my life, in my real world job, I depended on this tool. Old habits are hard to break, but this is still the best way to measure a round object.

Given the delicate shape of the house, I am making the finial in proportion. Make sure your cuts are clean, as there is very little chance of sanding out any large imperfections.

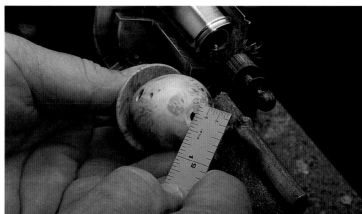

Recheck the size of the flat that will mate to the finial on the body. We want the finial to look like it was made for this, rather than haphazardly put on. Make the finial fit the house.

I'm cutting the tenon with a parting tool. This is for the 3/16" diameter hole we drilled in the bottom of the body. Needless to say, this will need to fit the hole reasonably snug.

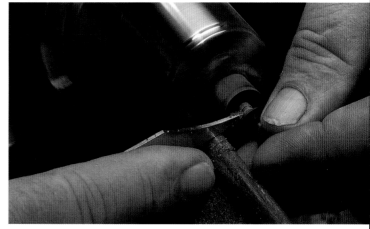

Parting off our finished finial. Arrghh! The best laid plans of mice and men. My mind must have been somewhere else…I have forgotten to sand and finish the finial. Well, maybe this isn't such a bad thing as sooner or later it's going to happen to you. Let's see if we can remedy my mistake.

I have surfaced off the end of the existing blank.

Using a 3/16" dia. drill bit, take care and align the tailstock as we did previously – we need as true a hole as we can get. Drill the hole for the finial tenon.

If you've drilled a clean hole, and if your tenon was sized properly, the finial should slide snugly into the hole with the mating surface tightly against that cleaned up area on the block. Mine does. If the tenon is slightly loose and will not drive (lack of friction), sometimes the addition of a little spit on the tenon will be enough to increase the hold, allowing you to refinish the finial.

NOW I am sanding out the finial, being cautious not to sand out any detail.

Now apply finish as before. This is how you dig yourself out of a hole. It has been said that a craftsman is not a person who just makes things, but a person who can overcome adversities in the process.

Our finial is finally sanded, finished, and temporarily seated to the house.

I have pulled out a little more stock from the chuck, cut off the portion that had the hole in it, and am reducing it to a round in preparation for making the perch.

Clean up the end to your liking. I use a 1/4" gouge and cut to a point for decorative purposes. However, it could be a round, perfectly square, or any shape your mind can conceive.

Turn the diameter down to 1/8", which is the diameter we used for the perch hole. I am using a small skew for this.

I normally do not need to sand my perches; using a skew gives me a good enough finish on this small object. If yours needs sanding, do so. After you have applied finish and are satisfied with the results, part off with the tip of a skew.

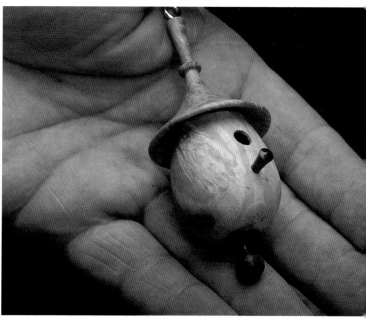

The birdhouse is almost done.

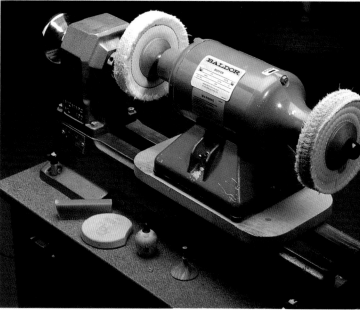

Our next step will be to buff and wax our entire birdhouse. We have already applied Deft™ as a finish, however buffing with a mild compound will smooth out the finish and applying a coat of wax will enhance the looks and give the birdhouse a silky feel. The reason that I buff and wax before gluing the house together is that once it is assembled, I cannot get to all areas with the wheels. I normally do not use the bed of my lathe to hold the buffer, but I needed good lighting during the photo shoot so some Yankee ingenuity and a little double-faced tape produced a buffing station. My buffer is a long shaft, 3600 rpm, 1/3 horsepower mounted on a board, which I normally clamp to my workbench. The right hand side has a concentrically sewn wheel; it is more aggressive than the left hand wheel, which is a loose cloth wheel for waxing.

The right hand wheel, or the concentrically sewn one, is charged with a compound such as tripoli or rouge. Avoid using emery or any of the coarser compounds, as they are meant for metal and are too aggressive for wood.

The left hand wheel, or the loose wheel, is charged with a good grade of wax, such as one containing carnauba, or a mixture of waxes of your choice.

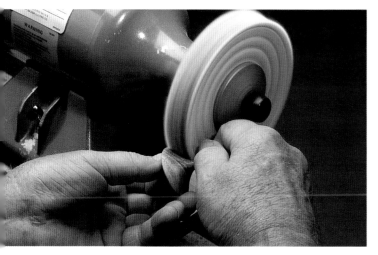

When buffing, always be aware of the rotation of the wheel. If you put a sharp edge into the rotation, I can just about guarantee it will be taken out of your hand, being a small object. I always buff or wax at an angle if possible, with the rotation going off, rather than against, a sharp edge. Another reason for buffing on an angle is that it buffs across any concentric imperfections and will help to remove them. Also, remember that your piece is not something that has to be buffed like a piece of metal. We have already established a good surface with our sandpaper. This is only meant to level out our Deft™ finished surface in preparation for waxing. Before buffing the roof, remove the brass eyelet for two reasons. One, it is very easy to catch on the wheel. Two, the compound will buff it and create a dark smudge from the brass that transfers to the surface being buffed. Unscrew it and save yourself some heartache.

When buffing the body, be careful of the entry holes as they may have a tendency to grab on you. Also, there is no need to buff the mating surface for the finial as this will be glued. Just buff up to it.

In this picture, I am holding the edge of the roof *against* the rotation of the roof. This is just to clarify what I mean by buffing against the rotation with a sharp edge. This is NOT the way you want to hold it – refer to the other pictures for the correct way.

Waxing the roof with the loosely sewn wheel. Don't underestimate the friction grabbing abilities of a waxed wheel to remove a small part from your hand.

My first step is normally to dip the end of the perch into the glue and scrape a little off into the perch hole. If necessary, put a little more glue on the end of the perch, then position it in the hole to suit your eye. There always seems to be a small amount of squeeze out, so wipe that clean if it happens. Here I have already installed the perch. I then take the tenon of the finial and basically do the same thing. Insert the tenon in the hole and seat it, paying attention to which grain direction will give the best appearance.

Wax the body. I have found that the small size of the finial makes it difficult to hold in your hand. Therefore, I normally put it on the house temporarily and use the house to help hold it, being careful not to apply too much pressure. Do not do this with the perch, as it will be in the wrong direction to the rotation of the wheel, making it subject to breaking. Use your fingers to hold it.

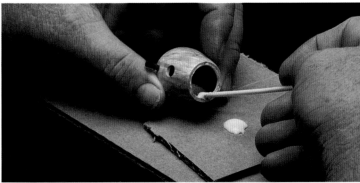

I use a coffee stirrer to apply glue to the inside of the tenon hole on the body. If you applied this to the outside of the tenon in the roof, you would have squeeze out to clean up. Position the roof and seat.

At this point, we are ready to glue our house together. I like to use yellow glue to assemble the birdhouse because any excess that gets on the finished surface can be removed by wiping it clean and not damaging the surface. With cyanoacrolate, any excess or squeeze out cannot be removed without destroying the surface. As far as adhesion of the glue, I have not really waxed the surfaces that are to be glued, although there may be some wax on them. Remember, we are making a miniature birdhouse, not a toy that a six-year-old will be banging around.

The basic birdhouse is complete.

Chapter Two
Basics of Design

What is design? To me, it is trying to create or conceive a pleasantly shaped object – in this case, a birdhouse. This will include not only shape, but also color, textures, and a feeling of being light in weight. Shape or form must convey the intended object. Color, or the combinations of colors, will enhance the form. The textures, the grain of the wood, or other materials used will add yet another dimension. Picking up something that is lighter than you expect it to be lends an element of surprise. All of these components in their proper proportions will produce a great birdhouse. The only problem is getting there.

Small differences are what make one birdhouse stand out from another. If you turn many birdhouses and strive to improve, you will notice an evolution taking place. Some features that you have on a house (either good or bad) will catch your eye. You may try to correct, expand, or eliminate them on the next house. As I continued to make birdhouses, my first attempts – which I thought were once quite good – paled next to my newer efforts. When one of my birdhouses really stands out, I study what makes this particular one so different from one that is almost an identical clone. I am not talking different woods or colors, I'm talking the form itself. A little thinner here, a bit shorter there, heavier or lighter at the bottom, etc. Pay

attention to the small details. Ask your wife or significant other to tell you what differences they see. Many times their observations will lead to improvements, as they will have a different perspective from yours.

Become critical of your efforts to advance your own designs. If you look through the book, you will see my own evolution. Some of the shapes I started with, which I thought were good, are now stepping stones to a much more proportional, more defined and appealing birdhouse.

When designing, try something different; even if you fail to make what you think is a satisfying birdhouse, the cost incurred by the loss of materials is minimal, compared to a large bowl. If you have an error in turning (design modification), continue your attempts to salvage the piece. Some new shape, idea, or method may emerge. Also, practice never hurts – it expands your experience and skills. The worst that could happen is that your piece may wind up in the burn pile or garbage.

Occasionally I stand back from the lathe and allow my eyes to become unfocused. This takes away the sharpness of the turning and I will sometimes see a slightly different image, which I can then expand on. Small differences are what make one birdhouse stand out from another.

On the left is a common sized blank. The four shapes illustrated are derived from this common sized blank. Each has a different hole drilled for the roof: 1", 7/8", 3/4", and 5/8" diameters. By maintaining the major diameter of the outside of the blank (kept as large as possible) in relation to the holes drilled for the roof, we create four totally different forms as we shape the birdhouse. With the small size of our birdhouses, even a small amount of change will affect the end result.

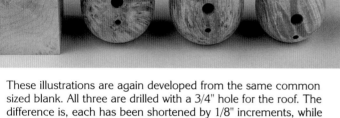

These illustrations are again developed from the same common sized blank. All three are drilled with a 3/4" hole for the roof. The difference is, each has been shortened by 1/8" increments, while still maintaining the major diameter during shaping. Here are three shapes that again are differing from each other.

So how do we accomplish this? Start by turning the blank to a cylinder. This will expose the entire grain pattern and give you 360 degrees of options for the placement of the holes. Every piece of wood was once a living entity with it own identity, and each will give you a different perspective. The picture on the top shows two different types of grain from the same species of wood, each having its own character. The picture on the bottom shows the end grain of these two blanks. To help maintain the grain pattern you choose, drill your holes 90 degrees to the formation of the growth rings. As you shape the body of the house, this will help you maintain your choice of grain pattern as you remove stock during turning. After the layout of the holes is complete, they can be easily drilled using a vee block and drill press. The grain on woods with burl do not normally have defined growth rings. But, turning the blank into a cylinder before layout will allow you to utilize the placement of the most intense figure.

Laying out the entry and roost holes should not be haphazard. On a blank with straight grain, a much more desirable location and effect can be attained with a little forethought. By laying out the holes on the face grain, you can sometimes use the grain contours (depending on the shape of the house) to circle the entry hole. In this picture, the house on the left was drilled on the side grain, kind of blasé. The one on the right was drilled on the face grain, making it stand out. This house looks much better, as it utilizes the strong grain pattern to emphasize the opening and the overall form. Little tricks such as grain alignment will make a large difference between the two houses, even though the shapes are common.

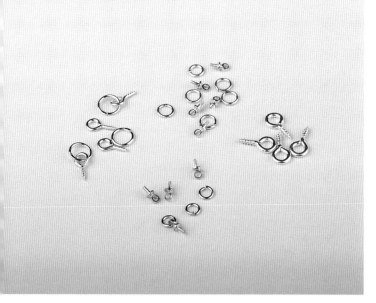

Most birdhouses require a means to hang them. There are many kinds of eyelet screws as well as eyelet screws with loose rings in many sizes. You can also use a straight shank fishhook with the gape cut off. The choice is yours. Mine…I use a #216-1/2 brass eyelet screw. I could use much smaller and neater mountings, but I had complaints on my Christmas ornaments that people could not hang them on some display stands when I used the smaller eyelet screws. Common sense also told me to use the #216-1/2 in size on both the ornaments and the birdhouses as I would only need to stock one eyelet. This may not be the smallest or neatest choice, but there always seems to be a trade-off.

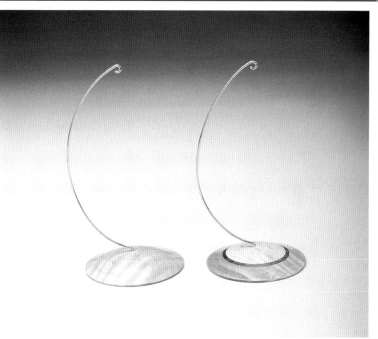

Birdhouses are displayed most of the time, not only on Christmas trees as ornaments. Commercial display stands are fine, but lack the creativity of the house they hold. By making your own stand, you can coordinate materials and styles to your liking. Remember, a good house has a solid foundation.

On the other end of the house, the finials always make a statement of their own. Play with different styles with different houses (Mr. Potato Head again). Sooner or later you should try one with a captive ring, as they always stir up comments. The perch (or roost), despite being small, should have some character of its own, rather than just being a stick.

Ideas, ideas, ideas. Some turners seem to always be at a loss of what to turn. It's probably a good thing too, or why the need for this book? I try to be aware of what is around me, and certainly for the oddity. For example, while traveling through Utah, the "Beehive State," I noticed the logo on the interstate signs. Voila! A new design emerged.

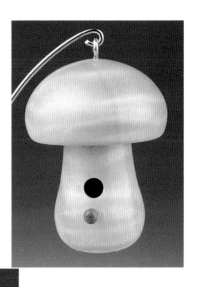

Fungi Flat

Who says there is any one standard for a birdhouse that is only large enough to hold the smallest of Illinois mosquitoes? Let your imagination have a field day. Beauty of form and proportion can also be incorporated into the whimsical. Look around you…there are many un-thought about residences just waiting to be created. Perhaps all ideas will not turn out to your liking, but the greatest sin would be never to have tried. If you have something on your mind, the subconscious works overtime. Some of my ideas have brought me out of a sound sleep in the middle of the night with a possible solution. Yes, it's hard to go back to sleep with my mind in gear, but I'll take it.

"The Dude." Yes, that is an honest opal I brought back from Australia!

Nuts to You

Distillery

Winter Retreat

Birdhouse architectural standards do not require that the entry holes be round. A small file can transform an entry hole into a statement, as shown here in Cupid's Cottage, Ye Ole Shed House and Hollywood Hideaway.

A woman's touch in a man's shop. Sometimes Cindy wants to be involved and has ideas I would not necessarily come up with, especially with respect to the colors she chooses. But, as you can see, they work in this group of houses that are "dyed to perfection." Did I mention that she is a hair stylist by trade and into color? Clockwise from back left, Sunrise in San Diego, Psychedelic Shack, Color of Money, Robin's Nest, Twilight Time, Little Red's, and Blue Moon are her creations and my turnings. A "house" of a different color, as the saying goes.

My normal choice is to always use the natural colors and texture of the wood itself as my canvas. Occasionally, however, nature does not provide certain colors in wood. To utilize these colors in your birdhouses, you would have to use a dye or stain. Aniline dyes, when applied sparsely over figured woods, can create a riot of color and enhance some woods. This opens a whole new dimension in finishing. I am not against coloration, as some great works of art use this medium. My personal preferences, however, still go with nature's paintbrush.

Occasionally an idea comes along utilizing a material that is not wood – in this case, deer antler. By incorporating contrasting woods with crowns (the part that comes in contact with the skull) and beam or tine parts, a unique house, "Hunter's Haven," was created. On second thought, being a birdhouse, "Raptor's Retreat" may be a more fitting name. I think I'll fly with it.

Chapter Three

A More Detailed Birdhouse

What are the reasons we would want to make a more detailed, or intricate, birdhouse? Egotism, pride in workmanship, the challenge of producing something unique. In my experience, people strive to accomplish shapes or forms that set them aside from others. Me? I am no different. I enjoy the challenge and satisfaction of putting together different woods and combining different shapes. I am human and strive to make a pictorial statement with my turnings.

On this house, we are going to combine box elder burl, satine bloodwood, ebony, and holly into a contrasting riot of colors. You can use whatever woods please you or that you have on hand. We will be adding intricate inlays, and outlining the entry hole with a contrasting wood. Come join the fun.

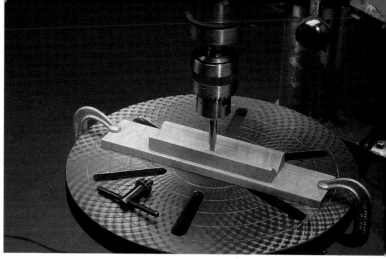

I am using a vee block for this setup. It will allow me to hold and drill a cylinder on a common center line, which we want for our holes. I made mine on the table saw from a piece of scrap. Use a pointer or small drill to find the bottom of the v, which needs to be directly under the quill, and clamp the vee block to the drill press table.

On this house, we are going to be more critical of where we put our entry hole. On the basic house, we had an option of any of the four sides, as the block was square. For this house, I have installed the block between centers and turned it into a cylinder.

The entry hole on this house is 11/32" diameter versus the 1/4" diameter on the basic house. The reason for this is that we are going to sleeve the hole and make a decorative inlay (border) around it. The final diameter of the entry hole will be 1/4". Here's an example of how to figure out the dimensions needed. If you want to end up with an entry hole diameter of 1/4" and have a 1/16" border around the hole, you would need to have (figuring 1/16" on each side) a 1/8" larger diameter or a total of a 3/8" diameter sleeve. Using the 11/32" diameter, I will have approximately a .046 border. Why? I just feel it's more proportional. I have drilled the 11/32" diameter hole approximately 1/2" deep. This will allow me to form the outside of the body without losing the border.

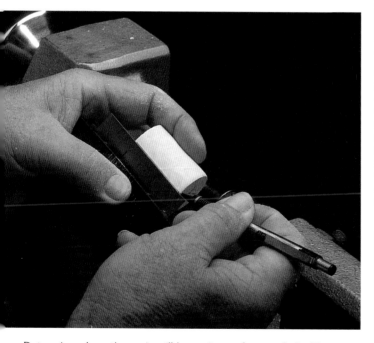

Determine where the grain will be optimum for your hole. This time we have a 360 degree range. Using a square, lay out your centerline. Determine the top and lay out the entry hole and the perch hole.

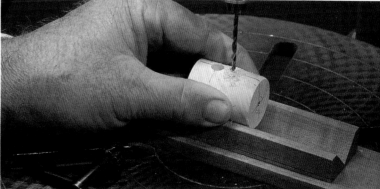

Drilling the 1/8" perch hole.

I have put a piece of satine bloodwood into my chuck and am turning it down to 11/32" diameter. This will become the sleeve for our entry hole.

I am drilling the body with a 3/4" dia. Fostner bit. I have used a depth of approximately 1-1/8". This will be followed by the 5/8" dia. bit. For that one, I will drill to a depth of approximately 1-5/8". Depths can be adjusted to whatever your design calls for.

Using a 1/4" dia. drill bit, drill the sleeve deep enough to fill the 11/32" hole that you drilled in the body. When the drilling is complete, cut off the sleeve using a small parting tool.

Now that we have drilled our hole, we can start developing our form prior to hollowing out the inside.

Make sure your sleeve fits before you attempt to glue it in. If it is too tight, you stand a chance of cracking it trying to force it into the hole. If all is well, glue it in with cyanoacrylate.

Hollow out your inside, using the 1/4" round nose scraper. Again, look through the hole to find your wall thickness. Be careful while hollowing around the inside of the entry hole inlay, as many times the wood is brittle or not glued sufficiently and will have a tendency to chip out.

Developing the form at the base of the body.

On this shape, I am developing a little bead and shoulder for decorative purposes.

Cleaning up the final shape using a shear cut.

When you are satisfied with your shape, drill a 3/16" diameter hole in the bottom for the finial and clean up a flat area for it to mate to.

Sand out the body and apply finish as before. The body is complete.

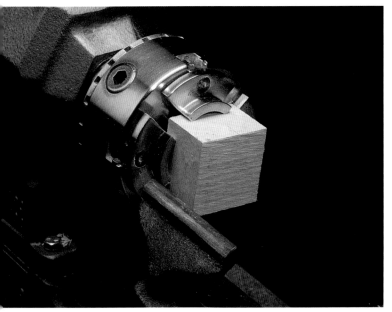

To start our roof, I am using a block of box elder burl, 1-3/4" square by 1-1/4" long, which was cut from the same material as the body.

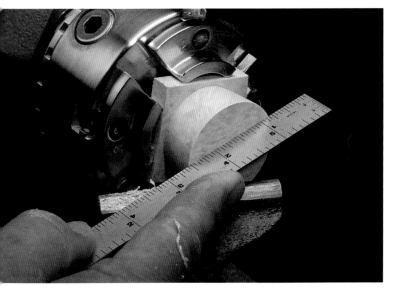

Reduce the block to a cylinder and face off the end. Use care when facing off and strive to make it as flat as possible.

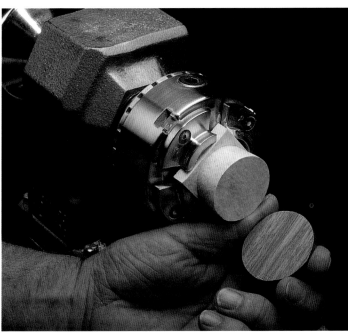

I have cut a disk of satine bloodwood on the band saw, approximately 2" diameter by 1/4" thick. I have also surfaced one side of the disk on my disk sander, as it will be glued to the surfaced end of the roof. We want to exercise precision when mating these parts in order to achieve the tightest joint possible. The reason we will be assembling and gluing on the lathe rather than stacking (assembling and gluing before putting in the lathe), is that this is the only way to make all the joints uniform.

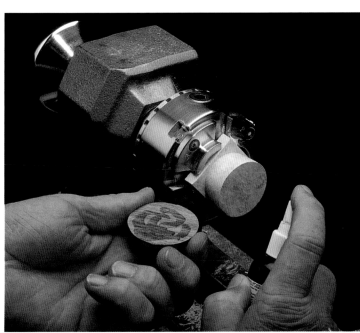

I have applied medium density cyanoacrylate to the disk and a shot of accelerator to the roof. Take the two parts, press together, rotate quickly to spread the glue, and hold together tightly. I do it this way (i.e., accelerator sprayed on before nesting the pieces together) because if you rely on spraying the joint *after* it is assembled, the glue will at times skim over and cure on the outside but remain uncured in the center. Using this method, the glue cures totally.

When the body is fit to the roof, establish the diameter of your roof. Here, I have reduced the diameter of my roof and the thickness of the disk to what looks pleasing to my eye.

I have trued up the disk and am starting to cut the tenon that will hold the body.

I have deepened the tenon to create an eave. I eliminated the satine bloodwood from my tenon because it was not needed. If the eave were not as deep as this one, however, it might still have been needed. I also took the tip of my spindle gouge and removed material from the center of the tenon to help make the roof a little lighter in weight.

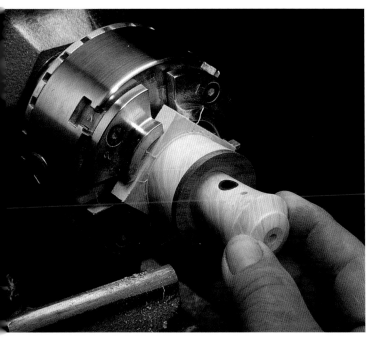

Fit your body to the tenon. At this stage, I use the satine bloodwood portion of the tenon to fit my body. As I develop the roof and create an eave, this tenon would become too long. The excess material becomes a guideline as I deepen the eave and continue my tenon into the box elder.

I have basically roughed in the eave and am starting to form the outside shape of the roof.

Sanding the underside of the eave. Be careful not to sand the tenon, as that would disturb the fit to the body. Upon completion, give the underside a coat of finish.

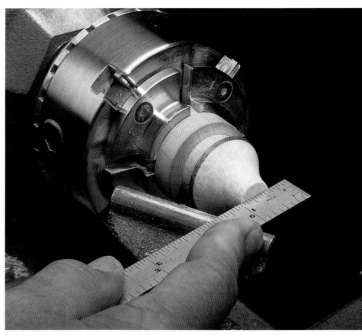

Face off the end of the roof, as we are going to start gluing on our contrasting woods.

Now that the underside is completed, shape your roof for roughly 1" from the edge and part off.

I have taken a 1/2" square by 3/16" thick piece of ebony that has had one side surfaced on a disk sander and am gluing it to the flat surface of the roof.

I have installed the jam chuck jig for the roof and installed the roof onto it. We are ready to start building the top of our roof.

I have lightly brought up the tailstock to give support while reducing that square piece of ebony to a cylinder.

I've reduced the ebony down in width to about 3/64", which creates a narrow band, and also faced off the end. It can be very difficult to see when working on a dark wood such as ebony. I just put a white paper towel underneath it to add contrast, which helps my vision.

Next we will add a piece of holly that is the same size as the ebony and has been surfaced the same way. Bring up the tailstock for support and proceed the same as for the piece of ebony.

I have reduced the diameter to a cylinder and the width to approximately 3/64". Earlier, I discussed the reason for not stacking before putting in the lathe. The uniformity of these bands is now apparent; if we had not done it this way, however, the bands would likely be uneven in width.

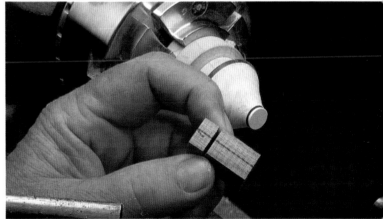

Our next step will be to add satine bloodwood. I have two pieces, one 1/2" square by 5/16" long and the other 1/2" square by 7/8". There will be another band between these two, which will form a bead. I like to try and have my grain continue as one piece, so I marked one side with an ink pen before I cut the block. The two ends have been bumped on a sander to make them flat. I'll start by gluing the 5/16" long piece into place.

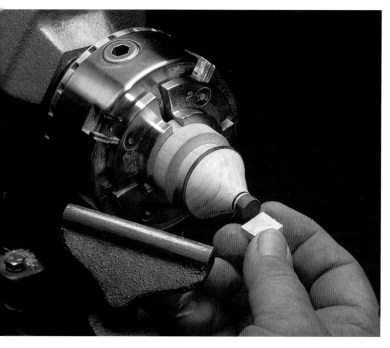

We've now completed all the pieces of our roof together. I have turned everything to a cylinder and, as you notice, I've left my box elder burl proud of the satine bloodwood as it will become a bead. I've also decided to cut off a little of the very top of the roof to make it more proportional.

I have reduced the first piece to a cylinder and faced off the end. I'm now ready to glue on a 1/2" square by 3/16" piece of box elder burl, which came from the same piece of material as the house and the roof.

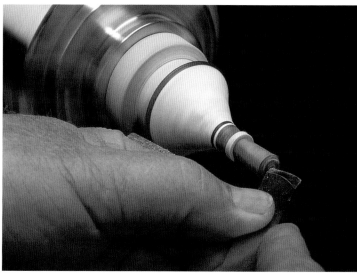

Having glued together all those small pieces, the small glue lines are not very strong. Chances are, we could fracture these joints without a lot of effort during turning. I am going to put a reinforcing dowel down the center, which should remedy the situation. To ensure your drill starting on centerline, use the long tip of a skew to make an indentation.

I reduced the box elder burl to a cylinder, using a width that I think will work for a decent bead. Naturally, this is not as delicate as the ebony or the holly as you want it to stand above the surface. Mine is about 3/32" wide. I then glued on the top section of satine bloodwood to the faced off box elder. I failed to mention earlier that when I glued on the first piece of satine bloodwood, I transferred the grain mark onto the roof, as I knew I would be removing it. As you can see, I have now glued on the top section in relation to that witness mark. Chances are, when using your eye and dealing with the speed of cyanoacrylate, you will not always get a perfect match – but if you never try, you never improve.

Drilling a 1/8" diameter hole for the dowel. Be sure to evacuate your chips often so your drill does not bind up.

Sand the dowel to a loose slip fit. Remove the roof from the jig for safety reasons and put a drop of glue down the hole. Start your dowel lightly, apply medium density cyanoacrylate, then rotate as you seat the dowel home. Don't dally.

I have roughed in the roof close enough that I can start taking my finishing cuts. The bead (being a piece of box elder burl that tends to have weak grain) plus all the joint lines will now get a saturation of thin cyanoacrylate to ensure there were no voids, cracks, or defects that I could not see. This is just to strengthen them. Better safe than sorry.

Again using the long tip of the skew to first make an indentation in the very center, drill a hole for the eyelet. This will ensure it being concentric upon completion of the roof. My eyelet calls for a 1/16 dia. drill.

Using my modified scraper to take a very thin finish cut. Be sure to blend the top and the bottom on either side of the bead so it looks as if it is one continuous surface.

Continuing to develop the form of the roof.

Finish rolling your bead and we're ready to sand and finish.

The roof has now been sanded and a coat of finish applied– it is now complete. Notice how uniform the width of the bead, all the spacers, and the bottom trim are. Again, if this had been stacked and glued before being put in the lathe, the chances of such uniformity are slim to none.

I have the finial pretty much to my liking and am starting to cut the tenon, using a parting tool.

I have put a length of 1/2" square satine bloodwood into my chuck and reduced the end to a cylinder. I am now in the process of forming the shape of my finial.

Continuing to shape the finial. Make your cuts as clean as possible; you don't have a lot of room for mistakes or torn grain.

Sand the finial and apply finish. It is now ready to be parted off.

Taking the long point of the skew, part off the finished perch.

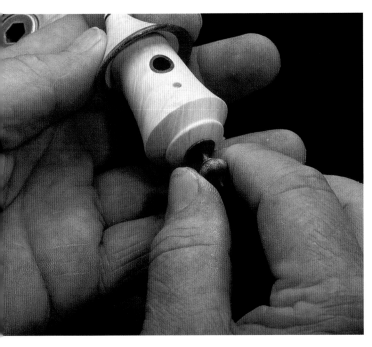

After parting off the finial, I'm checking the fit of the mating surfaces between the tenon and the house.

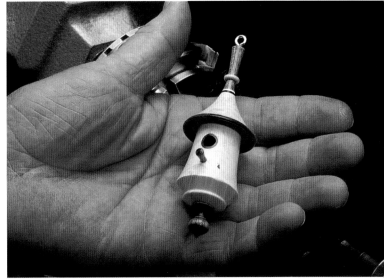

Starting to form the perch. I am using satine bloodwood.

The perch fits, so I have buffed, waxed, and glued everything together. This may seem like a lot of effort for such a small object, but the personal satisfaction of small detail work makes it all worthwhile to me.

Chapter Four

Pipe Dreams

Briar is a root burl. It is expensive and hard to get. It is also one of the most beautiful root burls available. A wood merchant friend of mine introduced me to pipe blank rejects. These are partially shaped smoking pipe blanks that cannot be used, whether from lack of material, voids, holes that would induce air, or reasons I am unaware of that would prevent them from making a valid pipe. My friend's original intent was to sell them for creating miniature bowls or the like. When I saw them, however, the bulbous body immediately popped into my mind as a miniature birdhouse. Voila! Briar cuts like butter. It is strong, sands easily, and has a satiny, leather-like quality. What more appropriate name for this chapter, then, than "Pipe Dreams." Of course, there is no law that says you can't use one of Grandpa's old castaway pipes as well – it may not smell the best but the memories it evokes will compensate for that.

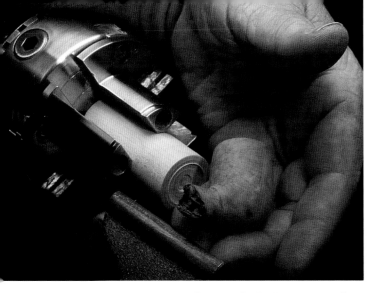

The material we are going to use. I'm sure the broken stem is why this one became a reject.

My initial step was to remove most of the excess stock from the stem area on the band saw. Put a piece of scrap in your chuck as we will need to turn a jam chuck to hold the pipe. Here, I have already turned a slightly tapered tenon that will fit inside the pipe bowl. Jamming it on the tapered tenon creates a tight fit. This will align and drive the pipe bowl for the initial shaping.

I have mounted the pipe bowl to the jam chuck and brought up my tailstock; as you can see, it is running true. Notice at the bottom of the bowl the shadow of the stem area that needs to be cleaned up.

I'm truing up the stem area of the bowl with a 3/8" spindle gouge and using the tailstock for support.

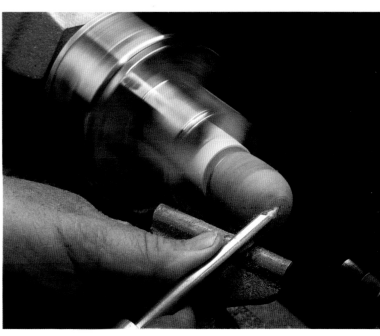

I've removed the tailstock and finished cleaning up the bowl.

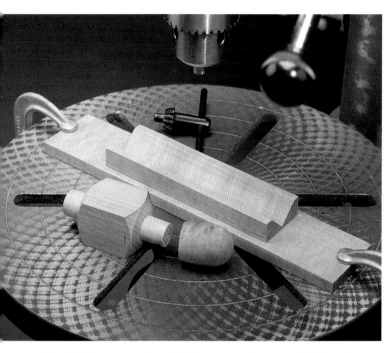

To drill the entry and perch holes, we need a way of holding the pipe blank. I have taken a 1-1/2" by 1-1/2" by 3-1/2" block of wood, carefully set it up between centers to keep it as concentric as possible, and turned a slightly tapered tenon on each end. The two tenons are of different sizes, made to fit different size pipes. I've found that these two tapered tenons will fit most pipes I've come across. I have also set up a vee block directly underneath the quill of the drill press and clamped it to the table.

Hold the jig tightly in the vee block, align with the drill to your layout, and drill the 1/4" dia. entry hole.

After determining where you want your holes to be grainwise, align that area with one of the corners of the block. Notice my scale – this would be aligning it with that corner. The reason for doing this is because the opposing corner will be in the vee block, allowing you to slide it and keep the same centerline for your holes.

Change to the 1/8" dia. drill, slide the jig in the vee block till the drill matches your layout, then drill the perch hole.

46

Using this method, both holes end up in alignment.

With the lathe running, I held the bowl against the depression in the scrap block. You can see the burn mark where it was hitting on the very edge of the block. I then relieved that corner with my gouge, reheld the bowl against the depression, and found no additional burn marks – which means the fit is pretty good.

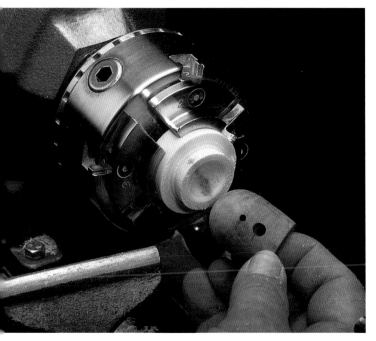

I've put a piece of scrap in the chuck and trued it up. Now I'm starting to fit the base of the bowl to the scrap block. This does not need to be perfect, as we will be gluing it in, but it does need to be close enough to make a good bond with the glue.

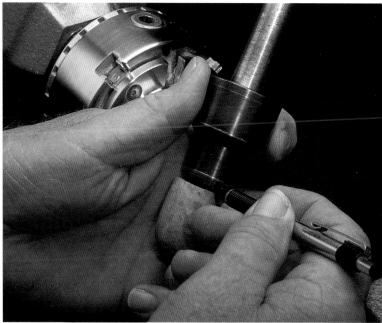

The tapered edge on my live center happens to just enter the bowl hole. This will align it concentrically to the tailstock when we glue. If your live center does not do this, you may need to make a small plug turned concentric to the live center to center the bowl hole.

Having drilled the top part of the house, I've changed to the 5/8" dia. bit and drilled the bottom half for my mandrel. As this is not solid stock (being a round bottomed hole), be careful when you're drilling the bottom so that you don't go *through* the bottom. Measure twice, drill once.

With the base of the bowl in the scrap block, and the tip of the live center in the bowl hole, you can see it is running true. Time to glue. I use the medium density cyanoacrylate liberally, because if there are any voids between the bowl and the scrap block it will help to fill them. Use the tailstock to hold it in place, then hit it with accelerator to cure the glue. It may be beneficial to wait a few minutes if you did not apply accelerator to one side or the other. I did not apply this beforehand as I wanted additional time to position my pipe blank with the live center.

Forming the desired shape before hollowing out the inside. If you do it the other way around, you'll never produce the shape you want.

The bowl runs concentric and it is now time to drill. I will use my 3/4" dia. Fostner bit first.

I found a void on the surface, so I filled it with briar dust and hit it with a little glue.

Using a 1/4" square round nose scraper, reduce the wall thickness. Maintain approximately 1/8" of the 3/4" diameter drilled hole at the top and some of the 5/8" diameter hole at the bottom to allow the mandrel to center and drive the house when we reverse it. Again, wall thickness is easy to determine: look through the entry hole.

Once the inside is hollowed out, start to remove the scrap block at the base of the house.

Using a small parting tool, cut the remainder of the scrap block below the house. If you look at the joint you'll see some uncured cyanoacrylate. Remember me talking about how if you spray the edges sometimes the cyanoacrylate will skim over and fail to cure on the inside? It just happened.

I've put my mandrel in the chuck, mounted the pipe, and trued up the surface. As I approach the bottom, I am not sure how much stock I have remaining. Drilling my 3/16" diameter hole for the finial will allow me to visually see how much stock is left.

I have finished shaping the house to my liking and am sanding it, working through the normal grits.

I've established my tenon and am making my finished cut in preparation for sanding.

I have applied a coat of finish and trued up the base, where the finial will mate.

After sanding and finishing the underside of the eave (again being careful not to disturb the tenon), I am shaping the top of the roof.

I'm truing up a block of apple that I've put in the chuck, getting ready to make a tenon on the roof. I selected apple for the color contrast. The two seemed to go together nicely.

Once the outer shape was roughed out, I parted off the roof from the remainder of the stock, put in my roof holding jig, reversed the roof, and drilled my eyelet hole. I am now further defining my shape.

I've refined the shape, sanded, and applied finish. The roof is complete.

I've put a 1/2" square length of gidgee in the chuck. This will be the material for the finial and the perch. I am starting to rough it out for the finial.

I have shaped the finial and am now establishing the tenon.

Sanding and finishing of the finial is complete. It is ready to part off. I will turn the perch from the gidgee as well, using the techniques described earlier.

The birdhouse is buffed, waxed, finished, and glued.

Chapter Five

The Branchwood House

This house is turned concentric to the growth rings of a branch, presenting a totally different grain pattern. It can be stunning. The combination of the heartwood/sapwood variation provides an interesting contrast. The wood that I use is dry, in other words, the moisture content should be low. If it is green wood, it turns very easily but will distort, warp, and possibly crack. I normally cut some branches that suit my purpose, seal the ends with green wood sealer, put them aside, and forget about them for a year or so until ready to use.

The wood that I am going to use is a 2 to 2-1/4" diameter branch of laburnum, a small tree that grows in England. I chose it for the sharp contrast between the sapwood and the heartwood. The length of the body is approximately 1-3/4" and the roof is approximately 2-1/4".

Take an awl and find the exact center of the pith on both ends. Make an indentation, as we will set up on these points.

The system I use instead of a four pronged drive is an old cup dead center. The cup dead center was previously used in wood lathe tailstocks before the advent of live centers. You should run a live center with a cup in it, as a 60 degree point would act like a log splitter when you applied pressure to drive the setup. This makes a friction driven work piece, which has the advantage of its slipping – rather than fracturing or splitting – in the event of a catch.

Using a 3/8" spindle gouge, I am reducing the branch to a cylinder approximately 1-3/8" in diameter.

Using a parting tool to square off the ends.

Using a layout square, lay out the centerline where you want your entry and perch holes to be.

Choosing one end, lay out the height of both holes. My entry hole is approximately 1/2" from the top of the house and my perch hole is approximately 15/16" from the top.

Position the body into the vee block, which has been centered under the quill of the drill press, and clamp to the table. I am drilling the 1/4" diameter entry hole.

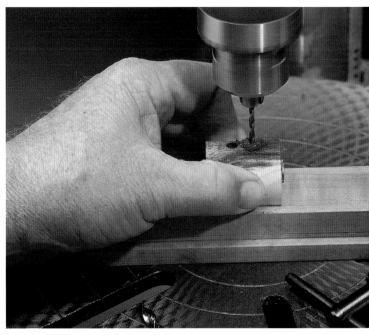

Drilling the 1/8" diameter perch hole.

I have reinstalled my four jaw chuck and secured the blank in it. I'm starting to rough out my form for the body of the house.

On this house, I have decided to use a different design. My initial hole for the roof is 1" in diameter. This house will taper towards the bottom, so I can't go too deep or I will run out of material. I have drilled my hole approximately 1/2" deep.

Using the 5/8" dia. Fostner bit, I am drilling approximately 1-1/4" deep.

I have roughed in the form and am ready to hollow out the interior.

I'm using a 1/4" round nose scraper for the hollowing.

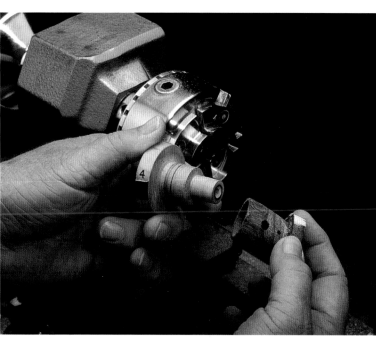

Since I am now using a 1" diameter at the top, but still a 5/8" diameter at the bottom, I need a different mandrel. In other words, this one is made to hold 1" and 5/8" diameters. I make my mandrels with care, and use them many times. If you'll notice, I have the jaws marked so they always go back into the chuck in the same position and therefore run true.

The mandrel has been put in the chuck, the body has been mounted, and the tailstock brought up to give support.

I've removed the mandrel and body and put in a piece of maple burl, which was handy and contrasted nicely. I reduced a section of it down to 5/8" diameter.

Reducing excess material and developing the shape at the bottom.

Using a parting tool, I am parting off enough to insert and glue into the body, which will let me carry out the form I intended to make in the first place.

Remember that measure twice, cut once? Somehow I missed 1/8" and cut off the bottom of the house. For the book, this may actually be fortuitous instead of catastrophic (i.e., a blessing in disguise). In layman's terms…I can show you how to repair a mistake.

I have put the mandrel and body back into the chuck and inserted the plug into the unintended void. I then pulled the body away from the mandrel so I had approximately a 1/8" gap at the bottom back to the end of the mandrel. I inserted the plug so that it contacted the mandrel and marked a witness line with a pencil for depth. (I pulled it out slightly so it would show up better in the photograph.) I will remove the body from the mandrel and use this line to set the depth of the plug while gluing. Yes, remove it from the mandrel or you will end up cutting it off of the mandrel.

Gluing the plug in also has its tricks. I put the medium density glue on the plug, then inserted it into the body to the depth of the witness line. This pushed all the excess glue to the outside end of the body. I sprayed accelerator on the inside of the hole to seal any glue that may come through. I then went around the joint line on the outside of the plug and body with the thin density glue and hit it with accelerator. With a little care, as you can see here, the inside will remain clean and still run true to the mandrel.

I have put the roof stock between centers, using the same location and drive system as we did for the body.

I've finished turning my shape, which blended in the plug to the body. I am ready to sand.

I reduced the blank to a cylinder and faced off one end, creating a dovetail that matches the jaws of the chuck.

Here I have sanded out the body, applied the finish, drilled the 3/16" hole for the finial, and faced off the bottom where the finial will mate. The body is complete. Note that we could have done this repair many different ways, such as making a plug from the same material, filling the entire 5/8" hole – which would have been OK. At times, however, creating a small band between the body and the finial (such as with this maple) ends up looking better. We'll have to wait till we are done with the finial before we know.

I have put the chuck back on the lathe and tightened the blank into it. I faced off the end and removed a little excess stock.

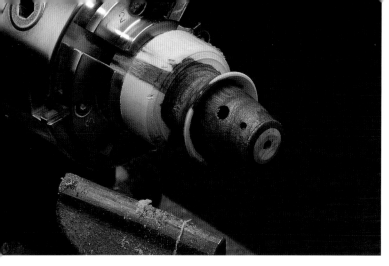

I have created the eave and tenon on the underside of the roof to fit to the body. I'm ready to sand.

The underside of the roof has been sanded and finished, as previously described for other roofs. I'm ready to remove any excess stock before turning it around.

I have put a 1" diameter roof jig (which I previously made and used) into the chuck and mounted the roof onto it. I'm now in the process of reducing excess material from the roof.

Looking at what will be the thinnest part of the roof, I see that I have a couple of small knots – which could jeopardize the stability of a small diameter. Therefore, I am going to insert a small dowel for strength, as we have done on some of the previous roofs. With the growth rings being concentric to the small diameter, this may also cause some reduction in strength. Use your discretion as to how thin you intend to go or how sound the wood looks.

I have put the dowel in, refined my shape, sanded, and applied finish. The roof is complete.

I am using a piece of gidgee to start making my finial.

Roughing out the finial.

When I made my finial, I took into consideration that we had a patch, or a light colored maple bottom. I left a ring that in my eye somewhat matches the light colored sapwood on the edge of the roof. Would I do it again? If I made a mistake, I would.

The finial after it has been shaped, sanded, and finished.

I've pulled out a little more material from inside the chuck and am starting to turn the perch.

The buffed, waxed, and glued house. One of the unique things about branchwood is that when you turn it, you never know what you're going to have until it's finished. The inside may have knots that have grown over, the sapwood and heartwood are never concentric…but the end results are unique.

Chapter Six

The Natural Edge Roof

To a lathe, round is normal. Any deviation from normal creates a mystique for most turners. To the layman, this is a foreign operation, a "how is this done?" turning. With a little thought and a glimpse of the techniques used, however, a whole new world is opened to the turner. Isn't this what we always hoped for? Use your mind and expand on this basic technique. We will be creating a roof on which the edge of the eave will be the bark edge of the log or branch. It could also have bark on it, although mine does not. Again, this is dry wood.

I will be using a piece of aspen, approximately 2-1/2" in diameter and 2" long. A finished roof has been placed in close proximity to where it was taken from a similar block.

My setup to drive the block is the cup dead center in the headstock and the cup live center in the tailstock. By eye, I have positioned the surface I want for the bottom of the roof facing the tailstock. I am also using the tool rest to align what would be the bottom corners of the eave; in other words, to make them uniform to each other. This can be done by moving either point – headstock or tailstock – to shift the block in the direction needed. Turn your toolrest around to its proper position and rotate the work piece to make sure there is no interference.

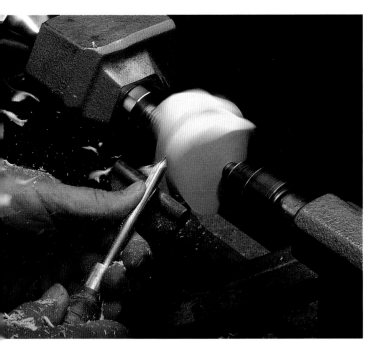

Reducing the block to a cylinder. Be careful, as part of the time you will be cutting air since the block is windmilling. Kind of float your tool over the voids as you cut.

This is the opposite side. Notice how these two points are relatively uniform.

On this roof, we have two high points and two low points. I am pointing to one high point. Notice the gap between the cut and the edge of the roof.

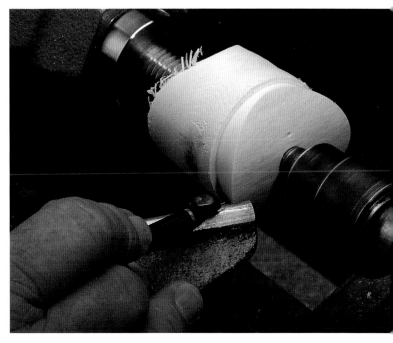

Using the toolrest as a guide, check the two low points. Both of my high and low points agree to each other, which means the shape of my roof will be uniform. I got lucky…even a blind squirrel finds a nut occasionally. If any of the points did not agree to its opposite point, we could shift the block by adjusting at the headstock in the direction needed, or at the tailstock. My personal opinion is that I like a uniform roof.

Reducing some of the excess stock into a straight cylinder, which will be held in the chuck.

Using a parting tool to cut off the end, which will seat into the chuck.

Put the top of the roof in the chuck, tighten, and make sure you have not disturbed the balance of the four points. If it is not balanced, make it so.

Starting to create a tenon to fit my house. This one happens to be 3/4" in diameter. I will use a previously made body to test the fit of the tenon.

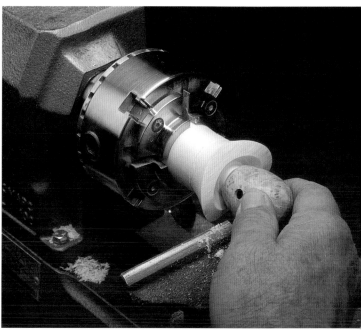

My tenon is just about right. The next step will be to cut the eave to my desired shape. Don't take too much from the eave area, or the roof will be out of proportion to the body when you start shaping the outside of the roof. Always rotate your work before turning on the lathe and make sure there is no interference.

Make the underside of the roof in proportion to the body. Remember, you are going to have the thickness of your roof on top of this.

Finish has been applied. Notice the sharp edge between the surface just worked and the outside edge of the log, which has not been disturbed. This has been our goal to begin with.

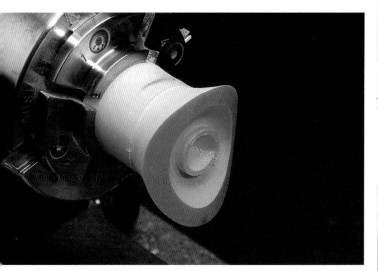

The underside of the roof is ready to clean up, sand, and finish.

I have taken a finish cut and am sanding the underside. Be careful when you sand, as the surface is not solid given its irregular shape. Notice how the leading edge of the sandpaper is held quite high, so there is nothing to catch. If this is not your idea of enjoyment, stop the lathe and hand sand.

By looking at the top of the roof when your lathe is running, you can see the shadow of the outline where it is not solid. The trick is to watch that while cutting in a normal cutting position. As you prepare to take your roof down to the desired shape, make light cuts to time yourself. Shut off the lathe, check your results, and adjust. This is not a macho cut...finesse and smoothness, again, are the keys.

I started by gluing on a thin blank of ebony that had been surfaced on the disc sander, faced it off to the desired thickness, then glued on a thin blank of holly, faced *it* off, and now have glued on a block of kingwood that had been faced off on the disc sander. All this for a little bit of pith. Again, because of the small glued areas, this roof will have to have a dowel inserted down the center.

I am pointing to the centerline pith of the branch. This would fall just about dead center in the smaller portion of my roof. I am going to shape my roof closer and cut it off at about the pith. The pith is probably the weakest spot in the entire tree, so rather than gamble I will eliminate the problem.

I have completed putting in the dowel and I'm refining the shape of the roof. I'm going to take my finish cut, sand, and apply finish. Before applying finish, take a piece of 400 or so sandpaper and lightly break the very edge of the roof. This edge can be too sharp and needs to be broken.

I've put my roof jig into the chuck and mounted the roof to it. I have also faced off the end of the roof in preparation for gluing on a piece of stock.

After buffing and waxing, the natural edge roof is complete.

Chapter Seven

The Bird Feeder

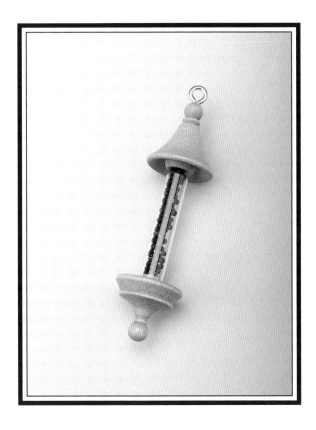

Now that we have been turning all these houses for small critters, we may as well feed them. Critters get hungry too. The wood I am going to use is Brazilian Satinwood, because as you know, finches love yellow.

I have bought some small test tubes from a surplus shop that I use as the seed holders. My test tube needs a 19/64" hole. Whatever you get for a tube will determine your needed hole size.

Drill your hole. On my tube, I have drilled about 3/8" deep. Your tube size will dictate what looks good to your eye.

Starting to form an eave and a little shoulder around the tube.

Using a small gouge, I am shaping the top. Remember you have a hole for the tube so don't be too aggressive or take off too much material.

I have cleaned up the inside, put in the tube to check that the proportions suit my eye, and am ready to make the top.

I have sanded and applied finish to the underside. Now that I have my shape roughed in, I am going to part it off, leaving a little extra material to finish the top.

I am creating a tenon that will be a snug fit to the hole we drilled for the test tube.

The top is mounted and it is running true. We are ready to finish our shape.

Remember the shoulder at the tenon must be cleaned up and running concentric, as the bottom edge of the top is going to nest against it.

Drilling the hole for the eyelet. Let's put the eyelet in temporarily to make sure that when we are done we don't encounter any unforeseen problems, like splitting. To help support the turning while you are finishing, you can bring up the tailstock and put the live center into the eyelet hole you've just drilled.

I have finished turning the shape, except for the very top. Pull back the tailstock and finish it off. It's now time to sand.

After sanding and applying finish to the top, I've inserted the test tube to make sure all is well.

Here I have pulled a little more stock out of my chuck and reduced that tenon down until it was a "loose snug" fit. Why? Being glass, test tubes are fragile and not all are exactly the same diameter. Too much pressure will have you looking for a replacement tube. Note that some test tubes have a rolled bead at the opening. These are much more forgiving, as they have more strength, but are not always available in the size you want at your local surplus store. When the tenon fits, make sure the area at the bottom where the test tube will nest against is clean.

Developing the form for the bottom.

Now that the top of the feeder's dish portion is complete, sand and finish in preparation for reversing it. Don't sand the tenon, however, as you don't want to disturb the set dimension you established. Upon completion, part it off.

I have faced off the remainder of the stock and am starting to create a hole for the tenon that goes inside the test tube. I'm using a small parting tool to make this hole. I am boring it to make a tight fit, to hold and drive the work piece.

Cutting a hole for the tenon can be challenging, given the small diameter. It needs to be close, but if it becomes a little loose, there is nothing that says you can't use a piece of paper towel to add a little tension. Bring up the tailstock to add support and start forming your desired shape.

Refining the shape.

I've taken my finish cut and am in the process of sanding.

I've sanded and finished the bottom. Other than gluing, the feeder is complete. Adding seed to your bird feeder can present a problem, as it must be small enough to fit inside. Kohlrabi seed worked well for this one, as you can see from the picture at the beginning of the chapter.

Chapter Eight

The Birdhouse Stand

Most of the stands you can buy have been mass produced in some foreign country out of wood that is unidentifiable and has no real character. Instead, let's turn a base that is worthy of our small creations.

I like to use a wood that either contrasts or blends with the house that will be residing over it. Here I have a block of fiddleback hard maple. It is roughly 3" in diameter and 3/4" thick.

The chuck I am using will not open wide enough to grip the diameter of the block. Therefore, I have put a scrap block in the chuck, faced it off, and applied a piece of double face tape. I have also surfaced one side of the block on the disc sander. This will give me a decent surface for the tape to adhere to.

If you have used a compass to lay out the diameter of the block before bandsawing, it can help avoid problems centering the block to the axis of the lathe – you can use the hole from the compass leg with the tailstock to align the block.

Truing up the outside diameter.

The exposed surface of the block will become the bottom of the stand. I am going to use an expanding mode grip to hold the work piece while I turn the top. In preparation for cutting a small dovetail for the jaw chucks, I have laid it out for diameter. My chuck uses approximately a 2" diameter, which provides the most contact and therefore the best gripping size.

I've sanded and finished the bottom and I am ready to turn it around.

Using my French curve scraper to establish the dovetail. I have cut the dovetail approximately 1/16" deep, because I like a thin base. I am comfortable with this because I maintain the jaws of my chuck (i.e., keep them accurate and nick free) and have a light touch with the tools. If you feel less comfortable with this depth, just deepen your dovetail.

Many turners have a difficult time getting double face tape to release. The easiest way I have found is to apply and maintain a constant pressure. This will allow the tape to relax its grip and slowly come off. If you try to use brute force or sharp movements, it just doesn't seem to happen.

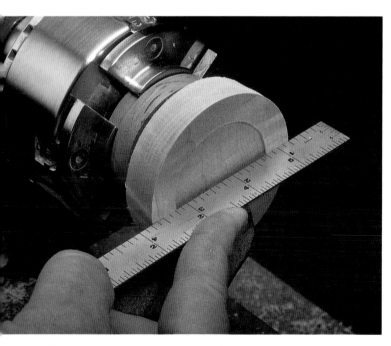

Clean up the base and the inside of the dovetail, as we will not be working this surface again. Mine is ready to sand.

I have turned the block around and it is now being held in an expanding mode. Be careful not to apply too much pressure with the chuck as it is easy to crack the block in this mode, especially without a lot of shoulder to grip against. I am roughing out the shape.

The shape is starting to develop to my liking.

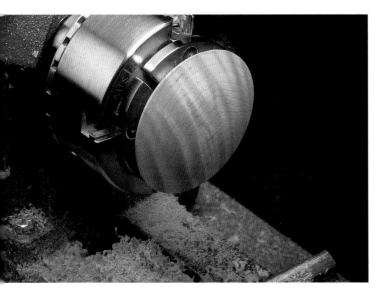

The shape is now what I had intended and I am ready to sand and finish. Occasionally, I like to create a more ornate stand, so rather than finish this one I think I'll just continue on and kill two birds with one stone (hopefully not the ones living in my houses, of course!).

We are going to make a decorative band of satine bloodwood around a center of box elder burl.

The first step is to remove the stand from the chuck and insert a scrap block. Face it off, as you will be attaching the inlays to it with double face tape.

After surfacing one side of the satine bloodwood on the disc sander, apply a piece of double face tape to the scrap block. Center the satine bloodwood on the scrap block to the best of your ability and hold tightly for a minute.

I have turned the diameter till it has cleaned up. I intend to keep the diameter as large as I can, which is slightly under 2". Here I am using the legs of the vernier calipers to check that the walls are parallel on the disc. When you are satisfied, remove the disc from the double faced tape.

I have now installed the box elder disc and am cleaning up the diameter. The diameter of this disc will determine the width of the satine bloodwood border. For example, if your satine bloodwood disc is 2" in diameter and you want a 3/32" width border, the box elder disc would have to be 3/16" smaller in diameter, or 1-13/16". Remember, 3/32" comes off each side, which makes a total of 3/16". Whatever width band you want, multiply times two, then subtract it from the outside diameter of your border disc.

I have reduced my box elder disc to the diameter that will give me a 3/16" border.

To bore for the inlays, I use a 1/4" square scraper.

I have relieved the sides and end of the scraper so that it will give me clearance, thereby avoiding contact with the bottom of the tool against the wall of the hole. If you used a parting tool, you would start contacting more of the tool the deeper you went, which would flare the opening of the hole. With the scraper, we can maintain a straight wall – which is what we want.

In preparation for boring the hole, I am removing the majority of the stock with a 3/8" spindle gouge.

Using the square nose scraper to cut the wall for the inlay. To help guide you in making a straight wall, sight down the tool and align it with the bed of the lathe. Take your time, as you want a nice fit. Also pay attention to the depth you have made the recess for your chuck. The noise of the tool making contact with the jaws can be very nervewracking, and needless to say, hard on the chuck. However, we still need to be deep enough that we do not remove the inlay when we finish shaping the stand.

I have completed the fitting of the inlay.

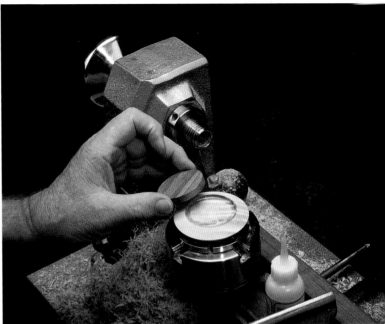

As the majority of this inlay will be cut away, I use medium density cyanoacrylate around the corner and the wall and do not worry about the center. Seat the inlay and use the thin cyanoacrylate around the joint line. This is necessary, as we are going to seat the box elder into this inlay, which will leave us a 3/32" wide border. If this inlay is not glued sufficiently to the stand, we stand a very good chance of chipping it out.

I have taken a thin parting tool, moved towards the center a 1/4" or so, and parted the center out of the inlay. Seeing how the center was not glued, this should pop right out. Be aware of it. We may use this slug for another project. Also, as long as we have this out now, you can run a little more cyanoacrylate into the bottom of the hole to make sure the inlay is glued in securely.

Developing the shape.

If you notice, my tool is considerably above centerline. This is not the normal cut with a scraper, which is normally at centerline. The reason I am so high is that the bottom left hand side of the tool does not come in clearance with the wall this way, as it would if I were much lower. In other words, the bottom of the hole would contact the tool if I were too low.

I have nested the box elder in and I am ready to permanently glue everything together. As before, I will put the medium density cyanoacrylate in the hole and use the thin glue around the joint line to ensure maximum bonding.

Immediately before taking my finish cut, I like to take a piece of polyethylene packing material and coat the entire surface with thin cyanoacrylate. The polyethylene material will not adhere to the glue and has enough pores to help spread it. With the inlays, we now have grain going in all different directions, which makes it very difficult to get a smooth surface on all the various woods at the same time. This process also makes sure there are no voids in the glue around the inlays.

Taking a very light clean up cut with my modified scraper.

Now you can sand…

…and apply finish.

Drilling a hole for the wire is the last step needed for the stand. The hole diameter is in relation to your wire size.

The completed stand with the wire inserted, holding a coordinating detailed birdhouse.

Gallery

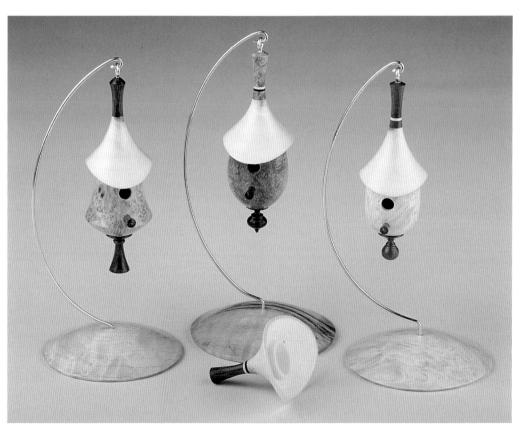

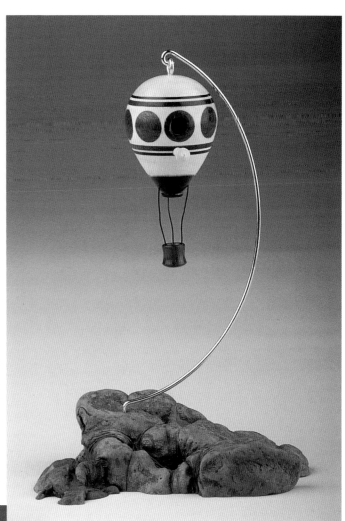

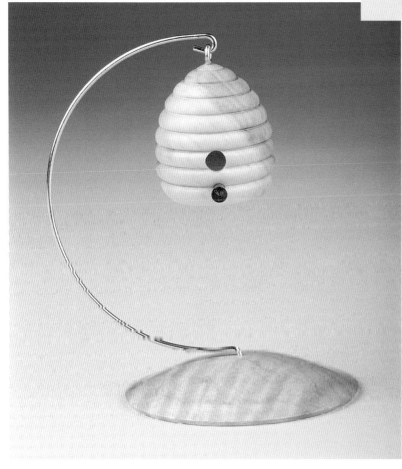

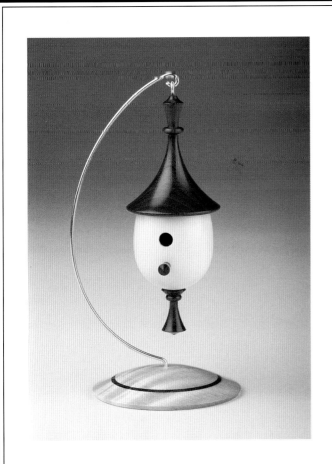

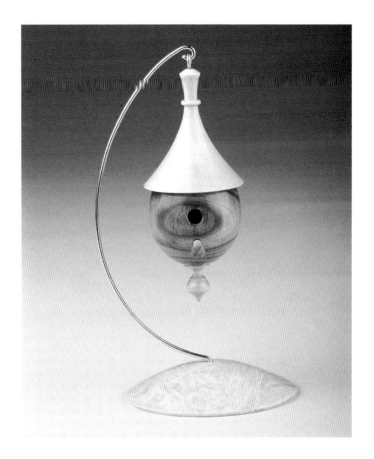

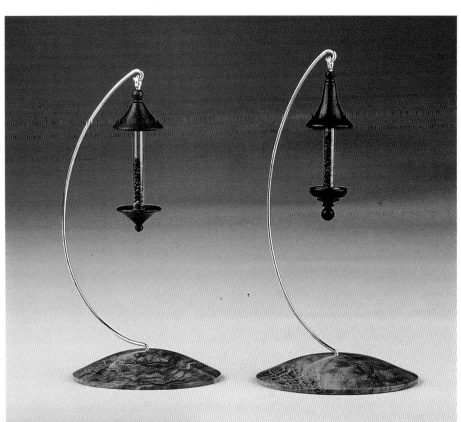